In Psychology I Trust: Boundaries & Healing

The Path to Authentic Living: Letting Go of Expectations and Embracing Your True Self

By Hari G. Darcy

IN PSYCHOLOGY I TRUST: BOUNDARIES & HEALING
First edition. March 27, 2026.

ISBN: 978-1972426012

Written by Hari G. Darcy.

Published by The Quiet Kitty Post LLC, 2026.

Thank you, Sista Long-Wind, for being the best mom ever (even though you're the only mom I have). Also, thank you CJ for being the greatest big sister ever and helping me with the kids. I love y'all both to the moon and back!

Stay committed to repairing the relationship, even when faced with setbacks or challenges. Consistently demonstrate your willingness to work on the relationship and prioritize its health and well-being. And if you're tempted to quit trying just remember why you're making this effort in the first place.—Steve Keating, How to Mend a Broken Relationship

A Letter from the Author

Hello and welcome to In Psychology I Trust series. My name is Hari G. Darcy and I am a developing nonprofit psychologist. It's nice to meet you!

For a long time, I was the ultimate caretaker. I gave to many people who rarely returned the favor, and still expected more from me. It took many years to shake off a lot of that negative energy that kept me from moving toward the life I deserved. I guess when you think about it, constantly having to duck and dodge ongoing negative energy is tiresome. You stop dreaming and love and faith in the lifestyle you are entitled to have.

Throughout my 20s, I've made unique decisions. I started questioning everything around me, like my worth as a young lady, mother, and writer.

Being a mother of five (possibly more) is truly humbling. I continue to do what is necessary to move forward—not because it is easy, but because of grit and vision.

Now, you're probably wondering why I'm telling y'all this now. Just like many great writers and natural born leaders, I had to step away from a lifestyle that served no purpose for me or my children. I had to re-learn that my value is not tied to how much I can do for others, but what I can do for myself to help others expand their way of thinking and perception. There were days when my body and mind told me, no, no, NO! However, I had to clap back and remind my body and mind that my spirit will NOT accept that.

Being a punching bag for years is not fun. Watching betrayal happen right before my eyes, and failing to call it by name haunts me sometimes. Still, I can't look back.

I will admit, I ain't no saint. Some folks really deserve my shoe size on their backsides (bless they crooked hearts). However, sharing wisdom through a psychological and sociological lens gave me the fire to keep going.

I learned more about my own behavioral patterns, accountability, and setting boundaries while healing from the self-projected hurt I was putting myself through. I even discovered new ways to soften my cold heart and allow my soul to rest underneath the delicate stars. Sometimes it's not about the pain that shapes the person, but the character building moments you allow yourself to go through just to be a better version of yourself.

Trusting the process is hard, and writing this book was even harder--but the process writing this book was (and still is) worth it. I trust the science and the art behind our

human emotions. I believe that, deep down, we are not broken, just simply untangling ourselves. This book is my way of taking the information that saved me and using it to teach you how to save yourself.

Before we dive into the book, please understand that I really want y'all to take your time. Love yourself during the discovery, re-discovery, or whatever you want to call it process. Think of this session as a collection of professional narratives and lived experiences at your convenience. I've included a lot of essays to provide clarity where many has failed us before (or came up with excuses to avoid offering the bare minimum).

Let's start somewhere new. Turn the page, and let us walk this path together--you know the healing and boundary setting path, and the wisdom needed to get through troublesome seasons.

I love y'all always, and wish you to stay safe out there. You're needed, you're valuable and adored. You're someone special, even when you feel otherwise. Thank you and God bless you and your loved ones.

Hari G. Darcy aka Mama Hari

Letting Your Story End Where You Choose

You can offer meaning without offering everything.

Many people misunderstand what privacy truly means. For a long time, I associated privacy with secrecy, avoidance, and even dishonesty. I held onto that belief as a shield, influenced by relationships where privacy was seen as an issue, not a limit. If I wanted space, it was questioned. If I stayed to myself, it was seen as suspicious —like I was cheating or plotting against the person I was dating.

That way of thinking didn't begin when I grew up.

As I moved into my teenage years, that pattern followed me into dating. My parents wouldn't have liked my relationships, so I kept them a secret to avoid trouble. I was looking for a change, something new yet worthwhile. I wanted to feel loved, appreciated, and chosen.

Most of my childhood was sheltered, so I didn't clearly

understand what healthy love looked like or how patience and care should feel in a relationship.

At the time, I thought I was learning. In reality, I was experimenting without guidance.

I didn't understand boundaries, and I didn't understand the emotional weight that came with certain decisions. Having multiple partners or casual relationships didn't seem like a problem to me because, from what I saw on television, it looked normal. High school dramas and soap operas made it seem like part of the experience.

But reality doesn't operate like scripted entertainment.

After graduating high school, I saw the difference. Life taught me how much privacy matters, but it wasn't a smooth lesson. My relationships typically begin on a pleasant note. I had nothing to hide. I leaned on the

person I was dating for support, and I gave them my all.

I cooked for them.

I cleaned for them.

I opened up about the type of love I never fully understood growing up.

I gave them access to parts of me I was still trying to understand myself.

At first, it felt safe. It felt like they took good care of me. However, that openness changed over time. It went from being vulnerable to being controlled. The ones I confided in messed with my story. They gave me advice that sounded nice but wasn't sincere.

They were pretty little lies wrapped up nicely. Their

voices carried convincing narratives that challenged fact checking. Listening to their truth, believing it through and through, kept me in place like a good little girl.

Somewhere in that process, I lost more than just my peace. I felt like I wasn't me anymore. I didn't know what privacy was anymore. Internally, I no longer felt like myself and started becoming who I thought I had to be just to keep the relationship intact.

When you're exposed to ongoing abuse and gaslighting, your sense of self can become distorted if you let it control your narrative. I came to terms with the fact that I allowed others to define how much of me was allowed to exist. I gave full access to people who hadn't earned it, and when it all collapsed, I was left trying to rebuild parts of myself I never learned to protect.

That's where knowing about and practicing privacy

comes in.

Privacy doesn't mean keeping secrets or being sneaky. It means focusing on living a structured life that best fits your needs, wants, dreams, and desires. For me, I learned that not everyone can handle my journey or need full access to my experiences to connect with me.

It took time to get there, though. I felt very uncomfortable because I wasn't used to practicing privacy. I used to over explain myself to where it got on everyone's nerves. Sometimes I would add on over-sharing sessions with a sprinkle of overextending myself just to feel seen and appreciated.

But when I pulled back, it felt like I was doing something wrong. Other people tried to paint me as cold, selfish, and confusing. Some even believed I was doing this on purpose, not because I was genuinely burned out

mentally, physically, emotionally, and spiritually.

When you're adjusting to a better version of yourself, you're going to notice a pattern in your life. You'll notice irrelevant conversations happening more often or unpacking things that have nothing to do with the moment. After the smoke clears, you may notice that it wasn't always about the other person, but how you're processing things out loud before confronting the problem within.

If I could leave this wisdom with someone, it would be this: processing your thoughts out loud and connecting with someone are not the same thing. Not all openness is healthy.

Vulnerability is intentional. It comes from a place of awareness where you pick to share something because it adds meaning to the moment or strengthens a connection

that feels safe. Exposure, however, is reactive. It happens quickly, driven by emotion that leaves you feeling like you gave away something you weren't ready to release.

If I could tell my younger self to slow down and love herself first, I would. Even though I cannot go back into the past and stop her from making poor decisions, I'm content with the experiences I lived through.

Going through those dark moments inspired me to write more, to shape, mold, and understand my psyche better. Sometimes I don't want to be here anymore. Some moments, I find it hard to look at myself in the mirror and call myself positive things and mean it. But I don't let that stop me from trying to do something nice to myself and my children.

I'm still choosing to move forward, not because of the roles I carry, but because I want to. Pushing through the

hurt, the confusion, and everything in between is my way of refusing to return to who I used to be. It's not about pretending I'm okay or forcing progress—it's about honoring the fact that I'm still here, still trying, and still learning how to show up for myself in ways I never did before. That choice, even on the hardest days, is what keeps me going.

Redefining Control: What's Yours to Hold, What You Can Influence, and What You Must Release

A grounded look at control, influence, and acceptance—how to stop overfunctioning, respect autonomy, and respond to life without losing your sense of self.

We often associate control with power, dominance, or pride. Through lived experience, control rarely functions as a linear or simplistic action. It can manifest as responsibility, urgency, fear, habit, or even affection. It can look like over-functioning, overthinking, or trying to stabilize situations that were never fully ours to carry.

People who are accustomed to holding everything together often believe that trying harder, overcommunicating, or enduring longer will eventually alter their circumstances. We convince ourselves that if we just do a little more, things will finally fall into place as they should. However, control has layers. These layers often show up as consequences, context, and limits. What feels manageable today can become overwhelming tomorrow.

Healing starts with recognizing that control, influence,

and acceptance are not interchangeable. Each one serves a unique purpose, and each one requires a different version of you. Understanding these distinctions opens doors to creating a life that aligns with your values rather than your fears, setting the stage for healthier relationships and clearer responsibilities.

At its core, control is not always negative. In its healthiest form, it looks like protection and balance. It creates environments where people feel safe, respected, and free to be themselves without boundaries being crossed. This form of control encourages guidance while holding space without suffocating the people involved.

But control can also become something else entirely. For those raised in unpredictable environments, control may become a familiar coping mechanism—an attempt to create stability where none existed. It may involve subtle

behaviors like gaslighting, belittling, or persuasive language that slowly reshapes how someone sees themselves.

There are several forms of control. Fear-based control triggers hypervigilance when one's environment feels unpredictable. Survival control appears when someone manages everything because no one else will. Protective control attempts to prevent harm. Habitual control relies on routine to create comfort and consistency. Identity control develops when someone feels they must always be "the responsible one" without proper guidance or support. These forms often share a common thread: life presents uncertainty, and a person struggles to gain control over what was never fully controllable to begin with.

People who grow up around controlling parents or

authority figures with unresolved trauma often inherit these behaviors—sometimes intentionally, sometimes unintentionally, and sometimes without awareness. In these cases, control shifts from power into the absence of alternative strategies for feeling safe and secure. Over time, these inherited patterns can also shape how a person raises their own children.

For example, single parents often discover that they cannot force another adult to become a parent. Readiness, responsibility, and emotional presence cannot be controlled into existence. A person may try harder, overextend themselves, or sacrifice their own needs in an attempt to shape the other parent's involvement, but these efforts rarely produce the desired outcome.

The truth is, you cannot control who someone chooses to be. Trying harder can become a form of self-erasure,

where you push yourself beyond recognition in pursuit of stability or acceptance. Over time, these patterns distort your reality and weaken your sense of autonomy.

Eventually, there comes a point where control stops working. Not because you failed, but because the situation was never yours to manage. You may find yourself pulling away, going against the grain, and reshaping your life without that person at the center of it. Their role becomes limited—present only when necessary, no longer foundational to your peace.

What becomes foundational instead is influence.

Influence exists in the space between guidance and manipulation. It creates environments that encourage growth, support decision-making, and respect autonomy. Earlier, we established that you cannot control who

someone chooses to be. When you attempt to do so, it becomes manipulation, not influence.

Manipulation overrides self-trust, distorts perception, and pressures people into choices that do not align with who they are. Influence, on the other hand, creates space for choice. The difference often comes down to intent.

Influence invites. Manipulation forces.

Influence becomes harmful when another person's certainty grows louder than your own intuition. Without choice, influence becomes control. Without clarity, control becomes manipulation. When you are influencing in a healthy way, you are not trying to control the outcome—you are offering perspective, support, and guidance, while allowing others to decide for themselves. That is not always easy.

When control is taken away, it can leave you feeling lost. If you are used to managing outcomes, releasing that responsibility can feel like losing direction, disconnecting from others, or questioning what comes next.

This is where acceptance begins.

Acceptance is often misunderstood as giving up rather than growing. Society tends to frame it as surrender, passivity, or resignation. In reality, acceptance is the ability to see things as they are without forcing them to be something else. It does not require agreement, and it does not ask you to shrink yourself to make situations easier to tolerate.

Consistent practice allows you to navigate reality with clarity rather than resistance. It helps you stay grounded while recognizing what is within your control and what is

not. For many people, control becomes deeply tied to identity. When it is removed—through loss, change, or emotional disruption—it can leave a person feeling disoriented or without purpose.

However, the only sustainable form of control lies in how you respond to what happens, not in the events themselves.

When you accept someone's needs—and your own—you create space for negotiation without forcing change. This process happens in stages. Over time, you learn how to move through reality without feeling consumed by it. You begin to stop seeking validation from people who were never willing to give it, and instead focus on aligning with yourself.

You create internal and verbal reminders to stay

grounded in who you are becoming.

If there is any wisdom to take from this, it is this: allow yourself to sit with moments that feel impossible. You do not need to control everything, and you do not need to convince anyone of your worth. Start with yourself. Move forward by choosing alignment over approval, and authenticity over compliance.

Letting go is not about releasing everything—it is about releasing what was never yours to hold. Being in control of your life and the story you are writing does not have to be linear or forceful. You no longer have to exhaust yourself trying to fix what was never yours to fix.

Because in the end, the only thing you can truly shape is how you show up for yourself.

Hari G. Darcy © 2026

Inherited Efficiency: Your Childhood Role is the Hidden Architect of Your Leadership Style

Decoding the Cognitive Conditioning And Intergenerational Patterns That Shape How We Manage, Delegate, and Regulate Under Pressure

Through studying organizational behavior—both academically and in practice as a former financial specialist—I've learned some unique things about how workplaces work. Well, workplaces *and* people.

You see, we frequently analyze a leader's "output" through strategic vision, like KPI management, and their ability to hit quarterly and yearly targets. However, jobs don't simply reveal who we are as professionals. They also reveal who we learned to be long before we ever stepped into a meeting room.

In most organizational settings, we evaluate leaders through **cognitive conditioning**. Some of these conditionings can show through sets of beliefs, emotional responses, and behavioral patterns from lived childhood repeated relational experiences. it's not inherently negative, just the brain's way of learning what keeps us

safe, valued, or connected.

What is Intergenerational Trauma?

Intergenerational trauma, in general, refers to the transmission of emotional survival strategies from one generation to the next. We frequently discuss this in clinical or familial contexts. What we don't do is talk about it when it extends into our professional environments and businesses.

Understanding intergenerational trauma requires a structured framework for recognizing *why* certain "simple" tasks can feel boring or difficult. For example, some people have a hard time saying no, or giving feedback, or even delegating responsibility. These challenges are not signs of incompetence, just reflections of early learning when we were smaller.

Why Early Relational Patterns Matter in Organizational Life

In developmental psychology, childhood roles refer to the adaptive positions children take within their family systems to maintain stability, connection, or safety. Our childhood roles merge through repeated interactions and various emotional cues. Over time, they become internalized templates for how to behave in relationships—including professional ones.

Below are three core roles that influence most leadership behaviors. Mind you, it is natural—if not normal—to have one, all, or none of these influences.

The Caregiver

In most jobs, there's usually that one leader or supervisor who seems to carry the emotional weight of

the entire team on their shoulders. They anticipate needs before they're spoken, sometimes volunteering before anyone asks. This is a prime example of the **caregiver** or **caretaker** role.

When someone grows up in a caretaker role, their attention istrained on maintaining harmony by meeting others' needs. As children, these individuals often longed for stability, yet their environment lacked it. To cope, they learned to manage both practical responsibilities and the emotional climate of the household. In psychology, this pattern is closely associated with an **external locus of evaluation**—a tendency to rely on others' approval or emotional responses to determine one's own worth.

In adulthood, this early conditioning often appears as difficulty delegating tasks, reluctance to trust others'

competence, and heightened anxiety when team morale drops. Dissatisfaction can feel less like a situational issue and more like a personal indictment. Their nervous system becomes attuned to emotional fluctuations, making leadership feel unpredictable or draining.

In these contexts, emotional regulation subtly transitions into a collective process, with the leader absorbing responsibility for everyone's comfort. Their efficiency is real but also shaped by survival learning rather than intentional choice.

The Peacekeeper

Not all leaders resemble the caretaker mentality. Some can resemble the peacekeeper—the manager who can walk into a chaotic meeting, scan the room, and quickly restore order.

Peacekeepers often develop in environments or situations where conflict is unpredictable or emotionally unsafe. Their nervous system learns early to stay alert. This pattern is known as **hypervigilance**, involving heightened activity in the amygdala, the brain's threat-detection center.

In workplace settings, the **amygdala hijack** is where emotional reactions override logical decision-making. For example, a simple disagreement may register as a crisis if the tone of the conversation feels tense. Many peacekeepers in leadership roles avoid conflict altogether, creating and slipping into patterns that resemble learned helplessness—the belief that no matter what htey do, the outcome will be negative.

The Invisible Child

Finally, we have the **Invisible Child**. The Invisible Child appears as someone who rarely asks for anything. At work, they don't request resources, even when they clearly need them. Leaders with this trait struggle to push back on unrealistic expectations or advocate for themselves or their teams. They, instead, adapt quietly and continuously until they burn out or are pushed out of the way.

Examining this leadership style closer, the Invisible Child trait primarily shows up in childhood environments where being overlooked felt safer than being seen. Over time, this becomes a form of **internalized bias**—a subconscious belief that one's needs, insights, or contributions are less important than those of others. In adulthood, this can manifest as chronic over-adaptation, reluctance to take up space, and silence in moments when their prospective is most needed.

Although this leadership style can be challenging to engage with, it does come with meaningful strengths. Individuals who lead from this role are often highly competent; their work is reliable, thoughtful, thorough, and consistently accurate. With intentional support—and training introduced at a slow to moderate pace—leaders shaped by the Invisible Child mentality can gradually learn what it feels like to claim authority, advocate for the resources they need, and influence those around them with greater confidence.

Rewriting the Internal Leadership Script

Fortunately, our minds are far more flexible than it is complex. Through neuroplasticity, the brain can form new pathways that reshape how we interpret situations, regulate emotion, and respond to stress. Anyone in a leadership or support role can benefit from practicing emotional regulation before reacting.

Why We Want Apologies From People Who Hurt Us

Decoding the Cognitive Conditioning And Intergenerational Patterns That Shape How We Manage, Delegate, and Regulate Under Pressure

Many people view apologies as a moral act, aiming to correct injustice, re-establish peace, or confirm our inherent goodness. Consequently, apologies transition from problem solvers to socially ingrained methods for fixing damages and restoring balance. In essence, we're conditioned to see apologies as a moral imperative, not a logical one.

An apology, in itself, does not resolve harm. Underneath it all, though, holds a much more thought-provoked psychological reality. The way the apology's expressed reveals something about the person offering it–their awareness, intent, and capacity for accountability.

Being hurt by someone is rarely confined to a single moment, nor does it affect only our emotions. The fundamental influence settles into the personal narrative we construct about who we are, what we are worth, and

what we can expect from the world around us. When that narrative is disrupted, the result is not just pain, but disorientation. The sense of coherence we rely on begins to fracture, leaving us in a cycle of confusion rather than clarity or acceptance.

A sincere apology functions much like a mirror. It does not erase what happened, nor does it undo the impact of the harm. What it can do, however, is restore a sense of alignment between what was experienced and how one understands themselves. At its core, an apology validates the reality of the pain—or even the fear of it—while affirming that the response to that experience was not irrational or misplaced. It reassures the individual that their perception was grounded, not distorted. In this way, the apology becomes less about the offender's remorse and more about the injured person's sense of self. It reflects something back that was, even if only briefly,

taken or called into question.

BUT...this raises more difficult set of questions...

If an apology functions as a mirror—reflecting our experience back to us—what happens when that mirror never arrives? What happens when the person responsible for the harm refuses to acknowledge it, minimizes its significance, or reshapes the narrative until it no longer reflects the original experience? What happens when the apology that was expected—perhaps even necessary—is replaced with silence, defensiveness, or a version of remorse that appears sincere but is carefully constructed for public approval rather than private accountability?

These scenarios are not rare. In the United States, there has been a noticeable shift in how

harm is addressed, how accountability is demanded, and how apologies are delivered. Public figures release carefully constructed statements, often shaped by legal or strategic interests, while institutions tend to respond only after pressure becomes unavoidable.

At the same time, social movements have brought long-ignored patterns of harm into view, while also revealing how easily apology can be reduced to performance. As a result, the apologies people wait for—or feel they need—now exist in a space of uncertainty. They may be sincere, strategic, or subtly used to regain control of the narrative. And for those on the receiving end, the question becomes less about whether an apology will come, and more about whether it will mean anything when it does.

We look for apologies when injustice occurs. We crave

resolution, fairness, and some form of balance in a society that rarely offers any of it cleanly. But what many people are actually searching for is not resolution in a legal or moral sense—it is confirmation when confronted. It is the need to know that what they experienced was real, that it mattered, and that it did not occur in isolation from a shared reality.

Across psychological, philosophical, and sociological lenses, apologies have increasingly become both a social expectation and a strategic tool. Their reliability as a form of genuine repair has not been delayed—it has been destabilized. When apologies are accepted without accountability, without change, and without understanding, the question is no longer why we want them, but whether they still function in the way we believe they do.

What begins to emerge is a more uncomfortable possibility: that we do not seek apologies because we want justice, but because we want to be seen—clearly, accurately, and without distortion. To be seen without dismissal. Without reinterpretation. Without being pressured to soften the truth for the sake of comfort, image, or convenience. What is being demanded is not politeness or performance, but recognition—of harm, of impact, and of reality itself.

At that point, the inquiry shifts. It is no longer about behavior alone, nor about the language of remorse. It becomes a question of meaning—of what an apology represents in a world where being seen is no longer guaranteed, and where recognition itself has become something that can be withheld, reshaped, or negotiated.

The Identity Rupture: What Harm Actually Does to Us

How Identity Rupture Rewires Self-Perception, Emotional Response, and the Way We Adapt to Pressure

Betrayal happens to the best of us. It shows up through neglect, dismissal, lies, or cruelty. The impact doesn't stop at emotion—it reaches into how we understand and hold onto the fragile structure of who we believe we are. Betrayal challenges the assurances we carry daily—whether we matter or whether we are simply worthless.

I struggled with this for a long time. Being non-traditionally married to someone for nearly six years can change how a person views the world when things go south. For me, I lost my sense of who I was and what I originally stood for. My beliefs were tested and ignored almost every day. I started questioning myself—whether I overreacted or whether I deserved the isolation after responding a certain way.

Clinicians often call this an "identity rupture"—a

psychological split that occurs when the way we are treated contradicts how we see ourselves. It is a disruption of coherence, where the self must renegotiate its own meaning just to exist or survive.

I noticed this rupture in myself when my ex-husband and I were expecting our first son together in 2020. I believed he loved me deeply. The beginning felt like a fairytale—walking on clouds, wrapped in a sense of home and belonging. I placed him at the top of my internal hierarchy—right alongside my children and God—believing that the devotion I willingly offered would naturally be returned tenfold.

Over time, something changed. The more I gave, the more I felt like I was falling short. No matter how much effort I poured into him or into myself, it was never enough. I found myself fighting for his attention through

artificial obedience and forced tolerance. Our home—no, our covenant—was never wholesome, God-fearing, or stable. At times, it felt like our relationship and the way we raised our children could be used as a clinical case study for what to avoid early in life.

Studies on social support suggest that when those we trust fail to validate us, stress increases and resilience weakens. I felt that in real time. I was constantly adapting. My survival strategy became adjusting my behavior, hiding my pain, and shrinking parts of myself so they wouldn't be used against me in future arguments. I did this because it seemed like the only way to keep the relationship intact.

I can still see it clearly. Before he walked through the door, I was expressive, open, and present with the kids. We laughed loudly, sang songs, danced around the house, and even had bubble parties when I overdid it with dish

soap in the kitchen sink.

Then the door would open, and we all assumed our position.

My tone, posture, and conversations changed instantly. Sometimes he noticed. It got to where I coached the kids to still show up for him—to greet him, to engage with him—without worrying about how I felt or what I was going through. I didn't want their perspectives shifting because they saw me trying to survive mismatched energy.

Over time, I learned how to make that transition smoother. I trained myself to adjust before it became noticeable. My presence softened. I went into hiding and started venting to myself because I no longer trusted the man I once loved and had children with.

Some days were heavier than others, and I had to carefully calculate my words and emotions to avoid unwanted questioning or hurtful remarks disguised as concern.

This lasted nearly six years.

From pregnancy loss to nearly being homeless, to being forecully moved into a backwater town hundreds of miles away from family, the kids and I went through it all. I had my reasons for staying, even if they weren't always visible to others.

For a long time, I stayed because I was afraid of losing him. Not the man I used to love, but the stability and resourcefulness tied to him. Out of all my past relationships, he taught me how to realistically and financially survive rather than go without.

He was the sole provider, and leaving without stability felt irresponsible.

So I adapted.

I endured.

I negotiated with myself to make it work—even when I no longer wanted it to.

One day, I confronted that fear directly and told it to get out of my life. I stopped worrying about losing him and started worrying about losing myself and everything I stood for. It wasn't an easy shift, but like many transitions in my life, the turning point came through my children and their declining mental and emotional health.

I didn't need perfection anymore. I stopped trying to

repair every detail for recognition or approval. The old version of me would have celebrated partial acknowledgment, believing that something so small could create stability and peace within myself and the household.

But I understand it differently now.

A sincere apology can interrupt toxic patterns of thinking and tolerance. However, its role is not to erase the past or undo harm. Its function is to restore alignment between what was experienced and what is acknowledged. When harm is clearly named and validated, the healing process can begin. It reduces the need for internal negotiation. The mind no longer questions whether the experience was real or justified.

The absence of that acknowledgment, however, forces

the mind inward. We replay conversations, rewrite events, over-explain our reactions, or withdraw altogether. These are often labeled as random behaviors, but in reality, they are attempts to restore internal stability when external validation is inconsistent or absent.

If I can leave you with anything, it is this: recovery does not begin with reconciliation—it begins with reclaiming the self you were always meant to be. When your stability is tied to another person's acknowledgment, it remains fragile. You become dependent on something that may never arrive.

Lasting clarity happens when you validate your own experiences, acknowledge the need for healthier boundaries, and rebuild self-trust without external permission.

Identity rupture does not only happen in extreme situations. It happens in everyday routines—in small adjustments and quiet moments where you feel yourself shifting just to maintain peace. The question is not whether you can adapt. You can. The question is whether that adaptation is costing you your sense of self.

Awareness does not require immediate action—just honesty. From there, the path forward becomes clearer, not because everything is resolved, but because you are no longer negotiating with your own reality.

That is where stability begins—even if it arrives later than expected.

Healing Beyond Forgiveness

How Identity Rupture Rewires Self-Perception, Emotional Response, and the Way We Adapt to Pressure

It is common for people to disengage when someone is unwilling or unable to meet them halfway. You may have experienced conversations that moved in one direction—toward agreement with the other person rather than toward mutual understanding. In moments when you needed space, reflection, or clarity, your needs might have been reframed as resistance. And like many people, you may have found yourself shutting down when you felt unheard or treated unfairly. These patterns do not make you flawed; they reveal how people respond when emotional safety feels uncertain or unstable.

Over time, repeated experiences like this can begin to shape how you show up in conversations. You may start anticipating dismissal before it happens. You may shorten your responses, avoid certain topics, or disengage before the interaction has a chance to escalate. What once felt like open communication becomes something measured and controlled. Not because you want distance, but

because distance feels safer than being misunderstood.

Different familial situations often highlight how people respond when their emotional safety is threatened. For example, when caring for aging parents, it is not unusual for generational beliefs about authority, age, or hierarchy to shape communication. A parent may assume that being older means being right, or that their perspective should naturally guide every decision. Conversations can shift from harmless dialogue into direct or indirect correction, leaving little room for anyone else to voice their perspective.

In those moments, you may notice a change within yourself. Instead of engaging freely, you begin to calculate your words. You may attempt to explain yourself, only to be interrupted or redirected. Or you may choose silence, recognizing that the outcome of the conversation has already been decided.

Over time, this pattern teaches you something important: emotional safety is not guaranteed simply because a relationship is familiar.

As a result, many people stop expecting mutual exchange and begin observing the relationship instead. You listen differently, respond less, and notice patterns rather than take part in them. While this awareness can be uncomfortable, it is often the first step toward understanding where change is actually possible—and where it is not.

Another example appears in your own responses. When situations feel out of your control, your reaction may shift depending on your level of awareness. At times, you may respond with frustration, tension, or emotional withdrawal. At other times, you may recognize the moment as an opportunity to pause, reflect, and choose a different response.

Both reactions are human. The difference lies in whether you remain in the reaction or learn from it.

This is where patience becomes essential. Not passive patience, but intentional patience—the kind that allows you to slow down long enough to recognize what is happening internally before responding externally. Patience creates space between what you feel and what you choose to do with that feeling.

Through that space, healing beyond forgiveness becomes more accessible.

Healing beyond forgiveness is not about excusing behavior or pretending harm did not occur. It is about acknowledging that some people may never meet you in the way you need, and choosing not to anchor your healing to their ability to change. It is the decision to stop negotiating your reality based on someone else's

limitations.

When you begin to acknowledge your internal responses honestly, you start to see the full picture more clearly. You recognize where your patterns come from—how past experiences, family habits, and repeated interactions have shaped your expectations and reactions. You also begin to see where you have adapted in ways that no longer serve you.

This awareness does not always feel empowering at first. It can feel stressful or lonesome, especially when you realize how much you have tolerated or how often you have silenced yourself to maintain peace. But within that awareness is also clarity. You begin to understand what emotional safety actually looks like for you, rather than relying on others to define it.

From there, your interactions start to change.

You may find yourself setting quieter boundaries, choosing when to engage and when to step back, or reducing the temptation to over-explain your perspective to people who have already shown they are not listening. It is normal to accept that not every relationship is meant to provide mutual understanding—and that acceptance, while difficult, can be freeing.

Healing, in this sense, becomes less about fixing relationships and more about refining your relationship with yourself. It becomes the practice of recognizing when something feels misaligned and trusting yourself enough to respond accordingly. In the end, you are no longer waiting for someone else to validate your experience before you move forward. Instead, you begin to trust what you have already seen, already felt, and already understood.

Honestly, that is where healing beyond forgiveness

truly begins.

Stepping Back Instead of Breaking Down

Breaking the cycle of emotional exhaustion and teaching myself to set healthier boundaries and loving myself first.

Conflict has a special way of shaking up someone's world. Even after the argument ends, the mind keeps replaying moments like a scene stuck on a loop. Over and over, we revisit what was said, what was done, and what could have been done differently. Without realizing it, those thoughts begin shaping how we see the world and how we see ourselves within it.

For example, when someone says something off the wall to me, I've caught myself responding with phrases like "I'm weak" or "I'm dead." It seems harmless in the moment, almost like a joke, but over time those words settle into the psyche. They build quietly until they begin to influence how I carry myself in real life. That's where it transitions from language to belief.

Many people learn to tolerate harmful behavior because it feels easier than facing the truth. They excuse broken promises, overlook disrespect, or reshape events

to match someone else's version of reality. Eventually, this becomes a habit. It drains energy, weakens confidence, and teaches the mind to question its own intuition.

Healing after conflict starts with awareness, but awareness alone is not enough. When someone keeps bending themselves to protect another person's comfort, they slowly lose sight of their own needs. It took me nearly six years, two pregnancy losses, and betrayal to fully understand how aware I was of everyone else... and how disconnected I was from myself.

I had to start small. I began noticing the subtle signs that something was off and chose not to ignore them anymore. It was uncomfortable at first, but I started setting boundaries with both myself and others in mind. Sometimes that looked like not oversharing when emotions were high. Other times, it meant not chasing people who clearly did not value my time or presence.

Over time, I came to understand that boundaries are not walls—they are doors. They give me the ability to decide who and what enters my life, and what stays outside. What helped me reach that point was learning to tune out outside opinions and turn up my own intuition and discernment. I started praying more, asking for wisdom, clarity, and truth. I asked God to help me sit with the feelings I spent years avoiding.

From the outside, I figured my transition probably looked inconsistent. One moment I was warm, and the next I was distant. I knew it confused people. At times, I wish they had given me more understanding instead of judgment, but I also accept that not everyone will see the process or the transformation for what it is while you're in it.

What matters is that healing creates space. Space to breathe. Space to think clearly. Space to see things as

they are instead of how fear or loneliness tries to paint them. When your environment becomes too loud, stepping back becomes protection, not avoidance. And that's where things started to change for me.

Stepping back gave me the ability to respond instead of react. It allowed me to pause long enough to ask myself a simple question: does this actually align with who I am becoming? If the answer was no, then I had to accept that no amount of explaining, fixing, or overextending would make it right.

Coming to that realization wasn't easy. It meant letting go of the idea that I could control outcomes by trying harder. I had to accept that I couldn't force someone to treat me better, recognize my worth, or see me clearly. I also had to accept that I couldn't build a peaceful foundation while living in a chaotic environment.

After a while, I stopped trying in the ways that were hurting me. I stopped overexplaining myself, defending my boundaries to people who were committed to misunderstanding them, and shrinking myself just to keep the peace. Real peace, healing, and growth do not require you to abandon yourself to maintain them. They require you to release the old version of yourself so you can step into who you are becoming.

I became more intentional about choosing whether the situations I was walking into deserved my energy, time, and patience. I paid closer attention to how I wanted to be treated in conversations and in everyday interactions. It wasn't much at first, but I'm grateful that making changes in my life didn't have to come from destruction.

Healing after conflict doesn't always come with closure or apologies. Sometimes it looks like distance, unanswered questions, and moving forward without

needing everything to make sense. It's about learning how to stay grounded in who you are, even when everything around you feels unstable.

If I could go back and remind myself of one thing, it would be this: I am worthy, and I am allowed to protect my peace at all costs. I am allowed to choose clarity over chaos. Growth is not about performance or transaction—it is about discernment, confidence, and the quiet decision to keep moving forward.

I Didn't Leave When It Got Bad–I Left When I Saw It Clearly

Understanding the difference between surviving a situation and finally choosing yourself.

Healing after emotional disruption is rarely straightforward, and it often raises questions we are not ready to answer. When everything falls apart, the world keeps moving even when something inside us wants to stop. True healing does not begin in the moment of impact but in the silence that follows. It begins when the noise fades and the reality of what happened finally settles in.

When the mind finally has space to rest, it does not always bring comfort. Instead, it replays events as if searching for a different ending or a clearer explanation. It tries to process what the heart could not understand in real time. It could be something as simple as replaying critical conversations, unfair arguments, or drastic relationship changes.

When I am alone, I often revisit my character building moments, thinking about what was said and what I wish I

had done differently. Meanwhile, the world doesn't slow down to match my internal pace. I'm still a mother, a college student, a daughter, and a budding business owner with demanding responsibilities. When I slow down, it feels like everything else slips through the cracks.

Professionals say the body holds what the mind cannot resolve, and I resisted that idea for years. Eventually, I had to accept that unprocessed disruption lingers like a toxic ex-spouse during tax season. It shows up in how we think, how we feel, and how we make decisions. Even simple choices begin to feel heavier than they should.

For me, my thoughts grow louder and harder to separate from reality. Old emotions blur the truth until doubt creeps in. I question whether I will repeat old mistakes or miss the signs of growth again. Living here, quietly living here, in that mental space becomes exhausting.

Every waking and sleeping moment can feel like an internal fight. There are days when I wish for one moment where nothing feels heavy. But wishful thinking does not create healing, and time alone does not fix what we refuse to face. At some point, the work has to begin.

For a long time, I did not realize I was responding to my past more than the people in front of me. I survived difficult moments, yet I rarely acknowledged that survival. My pregnancy loss stayed with me longer than I expected, shaping how I moved through life. The relationship I had with my ex-husband during that time made everything harder to accept and learn from.

He lived life on his terms while I carried the emotional weight of our home. We argued until sunrise, and I often said what he wanted to hear just to end the conflict. I was tired—emotionally, mentally, and spiritually. I prayed for escape because I felt trapped in a cycle I could not break.

During the delivery process, he disengaged. I cried quietly and learned how to hide it whenever he was around. I convinced myself that if I could just suppress how I felt, I could survive long enough to keep everything together and still appear "normal."

Back then, I didn't know any better. I stayed because survival felt like the only option. The kids and I didn't have a stable place to call our own, and the fear of being homeless with four children was real. He was the only person I knew who understood what it meant to struggle, and I held onto that.

I sacrificed my happiness and my sense of self just to make sure my children and I had somewhere to stay—even if it meant losing who I was in the process.

That experience changed how I show up now, especially in relationships. There are moments when I

hesitate to connect because I remember what it cost me to give so much of myself away. I am not willing to repeat that pattern, and I do not think anyone should have to. Survival should not be the foundation of love.

Now, I reflect instead of sinking into pity. I take accountability without tearing myself apart. I think about how often I overextended myself and how much I silenced my needs to maintain connection. Those reflections shape how I accept love today.

What changed internally for me didn't happen all at once, but there was a moment that made everything clear.

On Mother's Day 2025, I woke up early, wanting a slow start to my day. The night before, I said I would handle the house in the morning. I just wanted to move at my own pace.

About fifteen minutes into my routine, my ex-husband woke up and started pacing through the house. The look on his face told me the day would not be peaceful. The argument started over something small, as it often did. He assumed I was too tired to manage things, and I kept telling him I simply wanted space.

He was not listening, and the conversation spiraled into hours of back-and-forth. At some point, I stopped trying to make sense of it and found myself laughing at the absurdity. I realized the argument wasn't about the moment but about everything unresolved between us.

It was then something within me settled. I saw it for what it was. I stopped feeding into the arguments and trying to fix whatever was going on. Walking to the other room where my work-from-home equipment was, I packed everything.

No big speech.

No streaming tears and begging.

Pure silence.

I knew I was done participating in something that was no longer grounded in reality or respect. My focus shifted to my children–their safety, stability, and peace. I was ready for us to go home.

Looking back, I know I did not need to wait that long to choose myself. There were earlier signs and earlier moments where I could have stepped away. But I did not, and I have learned to make peace with that truth. Healing requires honesty, even when it is uncomfortable.

Now, I move differently and with more intention. I

remind myself to control what I can and release what I cannot. I cannot control how someone treats me, but I can control how I respond. I can choose when to step back and when to remove myself completely.

Sometimes, that is where healing truly begins. Not in understanding everything or fixing everything, but in choosing not to stay in what continues to break you. Healing means being intentional with your time, energy, and presence. It means refusing to attach yourself to things that do not align with the life you want to build.

It also means accepting that healing comes in layers, and not all of them feel good. But it does not require abandoning yourself to make something else work. You do not have to force connection or prove your worth to anyone. You do not have to stay in environments that make you question your reality.

I have lived that life already. And I am not going back.

About the Series

In Psychology I Trust is a collection of independent essays exploring human behavior, emotional intelligence, grief, communication, identity, healing, and the psychological realities behind everyday life experiences.

Rather than offering simplified answers or surface-level advice, the series encourages readers to think critically, reflect honestly, and develop a deeper understanding of themselves and the people around them.

Written by Hari G. Darcy.

About the Author

Hari G. Darcy is the creator of Hari's Helping Hands, a community-centered platform focused on emotional intelligence, communication, healing, psychology, and relational wellbeing. Through essays, discussions, and educational writing, Hari explores the complexity of human behavior and the emotional realities that shape everyday life.

Learn more at:

harishelpinghands.com

or

https://linktr.ee/harigdarcy

Hari S. Dary
March 2022

Book 2 coming soon!

I don't know how soon, but it is in the works!

Byyyyyeee!!!

www.ingramcontent.com/pod-product-compliance
Lightning Source LLC
LaVergne TN
LVHW052348100826
845147LV00012B/779

9781972426012